KAYDA-BUG

An Introduction

K. Lee

KLEPub.com

Kayda-Bug
An Introduction

Published by Krystal Lee Enterprises (KLE Publishing)
Copyright © 2022 by K. Lee All rights reserved.
Please send comments and questions:
Krystal Lee Enterprises
services@KLEPub.com
sales@KLEPub.com

To Reach the Author:
Email: me@authorklee.com
Web: AuthorKLee.com Social Media: @AuthorKLee
770-240-0089 Ext. 1

Printed in the United States of America.
All rights reserved. No part of this book may be reproduced or transmitted in any form or by any means, electronic or mechanical, including photocopying, recording or any information storage and retrieval system without written permission of the publisher except for brief quotations used in reviews, written specifically for inclusion in a newspaper, blog, magazine, or academic paper.

ISBN: 978-1-945066-30-6

Special Dedication...

I trust this book will encourage every young ladyto know their stories matter and you are not alone in your challenges. Let's live, grow, laugh, and learn together. Happy reading!

A very special thanks to my Lord and Savior for my purpose and life. I also wanted to say thank you to my beautiful children, Kayda, Akira-Zoe, Darren, and Ayden. I love you all and thanks for your patience as I had several sleepless nights finishing this book. Mommy loves you! Kayda, this book is for you, I love you always! To my beautiful nieces Desiree, Syeda rest in Heaven, and Angel I love you!

Chapters

Chapter 1 ~ 7

Chapter 2 ~ 15

Chapter 3 ~ 23

Chapter 4 ~ 33

Chapter 5 ~ 42

Chapter 6 ~ 50

Chapter 7 ~ 58

Chapter 8 ~ 68

Chapter 9 ~ 76

Chapter 10 ~ 84

About the Author~ 93

CHAPTER ONE

Hi! Have you ever been so impressed with someone you just had to tell somebody about him or her? You know, every time you see them you blush? This person floods happy memories in your mind. These thoughts make you smile whenever you sit down and reflect.

One of these special people that makes me smile is Kayda-Bug! She has been in my life for 12 years and I can't imagine living without her. My little Kiwi has always been a sweet inspiration. So who is this girl to me? My baby girl, the oldest of my 4 beautiful babies. I am known as many things: friend, aunt, daughter, and wife, but to Kayda-Bug I am Mommy!

Chapter One - Kayda-Bug

She has always been a ray of light to me. I remember when I first saw her in my dreams. I saw an image of my stomach and it was like I was zoomed inside my body. I saw the sack she lived in, the water around her, and the cool light that displayed the peachy colors surrounding her. I saw this image long before 4D imagining or seeing a video about it.

Her infant profile was so cute! It was like looking at a 4D sonogram. From the dream, I knew her face. I wanted to see her since then, but I was not always sure I wanted to have children of my own. I come from a family of 4 siblings on my mom's side. I also have at least 3 brothers on my dad's side. However, I grew up on my mom's side of the family. She had 5 children, 3 girls, and 2 boys. I am the middle child.

Growing up, I was always self-conscious about my appearance. As a young girl, I was very skinny. I was so skinny many thought I was bony. I think I weighed 64 Ibs in 4th grade and 5th grade. I wasn't a big foody but I did eat and wasn't starving back at home; although my teacher and school may have thought it.

We didn't have a lot of money, but my mom cooked 2 meals a day when I was in elementary school. We usually ate one or two meals at school, so it was a good break for my mom. Things did change as I got older and my mom went to work. I loved her staying at home with us, it was fun to have her attention all day and learn from her.

My mom and stepdad divorced when I was in

3rd grade. Before they divorced I was around all my siblings and parents from birth. I did not know my birth father as a child. He left me with a blanket and a glow toy I saw when I was young. As I grew older those items were donated or left behind when we moved. I did wish I could have kept them. I didn't meet my natural father until I was 30 years old!

Can you believe waiting all that time to see your dad? If you have a dad you see, be sure to tell him you love him. Daddies need love too! I love you, dad. The first time I saw him in person I flew into the Las Vegas airport. I flew from Atlanta GA to Las Vegas where I saw not only my dad but my Grandma Brenda and Papa Tim!

It was a great time getting in my Papa Tim's Duele 4-door black truck with silver rims. It was so tall, I had to jump up to get in it! To jump in I had to hold on to the handle near the door. The truck drove so smoothly that I almost went to sleep driving from Las Vegas to Kingman Arizona.

Wow, it was so hot in Arizona! It felt like I was in a desert. Surprise, surprise, I was in the desert! When I was in Vegas one of my dad's church friends gave me a rattlesnake skin! Boy, I was afraid to touch it, but the man reassured me it was dead. It felt smooth to the touch.

I kept the skin in a zip bag to keep it from drying out. I ended up giving it to my oldest brother because I felt responsible for why his snake died a few years prior. You see, I don't like snakes. I mean not at

Chapter One - Kayda-Bug

all, especially a few years ago. I didn't like any reptiles in fact at the time.

In Florida, where I lived before moving to Georgia, there are lizards that run everywhere! You can be walking down the street and see them cross right in front of you. I often saw lizards in the trees, bushes, by the pool, and sometimes even in the house! It made my skin crawl to see them.

Back to the snake, my brother came to town and he brought his pet snake. He would play with it in his hands and even let it wrap around his wrist. He would ask me, "Isn't she cute?" Unsure what to say, I said "Her colors are cute but I'm afraid of snakes Kelly." He told me she was friendly but I could not get past that she was a snake!

When it was time to sleep I asked my brother to leave the snake in the car, in her tank, and crack the windows. I was afraid it would break free and live in my house! The thought scared me beyond belief! My brother was sweet and left her in the car to cure my fears, but she was warm-blooded and needed heat. I didn't understand it at the time.

Normally it doesn't get that cold in Florida, but this time of year it can be a bit chilly. It wasn't summer but winter season so the overnights can be cold. So, yes it was too cold for the snake we found out the next morning.

When we checked on the snake it was as stiff as a board! It didn't move at all when Kelly held it. He did shed a few tears that he quickly wiped away. I felt so bad at that moment. I wanted to melt away like an ice cube under the Las Vegas sun.

My brother was sad but he forgave me and I wanted to do something for him. He later got a bearded dragon lizard and I love her! She is huge but I still think she is gorgeous. People can change with time and I am living proof. Once my Kayda-bug got a turtle and the crazy part, it was my idea to get him.

His name was Jacob and I loved this turtle so much. He was an alligator snapping turtle that belonged to the aquatic category. He loved to be in the water but could also be on land. I got him for Kayda's birthday as a gift. She loved Jacob too as well as her baby sister, Akira-Zoe.

Jacob would come out of the tank and walk across our hands. He would crawl up our shirts and I taught him other tricks too. He would follow me around and I strongly believe he knew his name! The turtle was like a reptile dog to me and he never made me feel scared or uncomfortable.

He lived with us for a year and a half. During that time he grew so much. When I got him he was the size of a silver dollar. In less than 2 years he grew four times his size. The turtle my neighbor's son had was half of his size and our turtle was younger!

One day Kayda-Bug and her cousin, Desiree, thought about giving the turtle a bath. He could get pretty stinky at times so I understand their intentions. Normally, I would take care of Jacob's tank and clean

Chapter One - Kayda-Bug

him off because his size did intimidate Kayda. She was very comfortable with him when he was small, but she grew more scared as he got bigger.

On this day something went very wrong with the bath they had planned. Instead of rinsing him under cool water, they thought hot water would be more comfortable for the turtle. Jacob was not a normal turtle, where he could hide in his shell. He was aquatic so his limbs were made to stay outside the shell. My niece and daughter thought the water was fine.

When I looked at the water, however, I could see the steam coming from the faucet. I told them, "Turn the water off! It's too hot!" Our cool turtle had gotten stiff within minutes. I am not sure how long the water was running before I walked into the kitchen, but it had to be for at least several minutes.

The hot water was hitting his skin the whole time. Kayda burst into tears as I checked to see if my buddy would move. He was so active and to see him just sitting in one spot I knew something was wrong. He just stiffened up and he died in my hands.

I was so hurt and I understood the tears my brother cried for a reptile. I too shed tears for my little reptile baby. I will always miss Jacob. We had a turtle funeral for him and we laid him to rest in a shoebox with a lid. Rest in turtle heaven Jacob!

Being pregnant with Kayda-Bug was fun. When she would move in my stomach, I could see the movement happening under my skin and it reminded me of how smooth the movement was when Jacob moved around. Sometimes she would kick so hard she would hit the table! When I was sitting down I started scooting back from the table because she clearly wanted more space.

It was a bit strange sometimes to think about how there was a whole human growing in my stomach! But my husband and I were excited, yet nervous about her coming into the world. Coming up with her name took us a few months to pin down. Luckily we had about 10 months to figure it out. Her father and I said we would give a boy a name that started with the letter "D" and a girl the letter "K." At first we were mostly planning boy names.

I knew from my dream but we didn't have a doctor's confirmation to know we were having a girl until 5 months into our pregnancy. We had to wait until we did our 20-week ultrasound. I remember I was in the room with my baby sister, Kayda-Bug's aunt, Ebony. She saw her kicking in my stomach and guess what, she had her two middle fingers in her mouth! She was such a busy baby in my stomach.

My baby sister loved Kayda so much. She was my first babysitter and she could get her to stop crying without milk. I got plenty of sleep when Kayda was a newborn because of my baby sister.

My older sister taught me how to be patient. I grew up around my nieces, Desiree and Syeda. I loved watching my older sister, Nikki care for them, cook, and teach them. I treated my nieces like they were my kids

Chapter One - Kayda-Bug
when I would watch them growing up.

CHAPTER TWO

I remember taking my eldest niece Desiree to SeaWorld when she was 3 years old. She had so much fun with me that day and guess what? She still remembers it to this day. She is in her twenties now. I had so much fun with her on that day. She made me smile and laugh as we went from event to event. I loved the brown almond eyes she had that looked so bright and happy as she saw the animals do tricks. Her favorite show that day was not the animals that swam but the dog show!

She loved the dog show so much, that I walked her up to the stage when the show ended to pet the dogs. She loved the fluffy white Pyrenees inside the show. All the animals, ducks, cats, dogs, and even birds

Chapter Two - Kayda-Bug

were rescued animals. Kayda looked at the show with great enthusiasm. She was happy to take pictures with that large dog but we had to move on so they could set up for the next show.

Walking away from that stage was very difficult. I had to pick her up and throw her over my shoulders as she kicked and cried all the way out of the theater. Once I got her outside, I strapped her into her stroller and bribed her with ice cream to stop crying. She was happy to have her cone but she still remembered that pretty dog! I did too.

These two beautiful sisters of mine were both there when my cutie was born along with my mother. It took over 35 hours for my daughter to make her way into the world! I remember I had terrible pain, so strong it had me lying on the floor. I was balled up like I had a terrible stomach ache.

I called my eldest sister and she came to find me at home. Nikki and Ebony were already together, so we three left for the hospital together. They both seemed to take forever to get there. Nikki came into the house with Ebony's key, and she said, "Krystal, are you ready to go to the hospital?" I responded, "I think so," as I swooned in pain. I wasn't sure if the pain I felt was the real thing or Braxton Hicks, which are practice labor pains.

We all loaded up into the car and Nikki drove us to the hospital. My mom came many hours later, in fact, it was the next day. I was in labor for more than a day but when I arrived at the hospital I still had another 15 hours or so to go. You have to get to 10 centimeters dilated before you can have a baby.

I was at 4 centimeters for like 20 hours. The only way I could get admitted to the hospital was if I was 5 centimeters or more. So I remember walking with my sisters outside the hospital for at least 2 hours before I was admitted.

They took shifts staying up with me for 24 hours. Then the two of them got help when my mom came. She knew from the start I had many more hours to go and she was right! When my mom came I had only gotten to 7 centimeters all those hours later.

The nurses told me if Kayda didn't come out in the next hour I would have to get a c-section. That's a surgery to remove the baby by entering the stomach. I was scared but my mom said, "We ain't going to do that."

My mom encouraged me and stopped me from panicking. She started to pray and we all participated. My sisters, our mom, and I had a good session that day. It was so good I forgot I was in labor lol! I felt Yah/God enter that room on Labor Day 2009.

It seemed like as soon as we finished praying the nurse entered the room to see if I had reached 10. At that moment I was at 9 centimeters and she told me not to push. I couldn't help it though. Not even 45 minutes later she came back to check and I was 10 centimeters.

Kayda-Bug was coming and no one could hold her back. The doctor had not made it yet because she

Chapter Two - Kayda-Bug

assumed I had more time because of how slow I was moving these last two days. My doctor was rushing and my mom and sisters talked me through it all.

I was so grateful for their patience with me. My husband at the time was out of the country on military duty and I was afraid to deliver Kayda by myself. I thanked Yah/God for them.

My doctor finally made it and when she came in I was already pushing with the nurses present. And just like that, within 10 minutes and 3 pushes, my daughter was here! She came out asleep and sucking on her two middle fingers. The same way we saw her in the womb was how she was born. She was born at 9:35 pm. The nurse took the baby and wiped her off and she was still asleep!

She didn't wake up until she got her foot pricked. She woke up letting out one cry and went back to sleep. She had us all tickled from the first moment she entered the Earth! I held her along with my sisters and mother for a little bit before she was taken off for her first bath. My mom has always been protective of her children. She was protective of Kayda-Bug too I quickly found out! I remember she told the nurse if she kept scrubbing Kayda as hard as she was, she was going to bathe Kayda herself!

I was so tickled by it. You cannot mess with a grandbaby with a grandma watching. The nurse seemed to ignore her so my mom intercepted the bathing process, and gave Kayda-Bug her first bath. Technically, Kayda still hadn't gotten her nickname, Kayda-Bug yet. It wasn't until Kayda took her first pictures the next morning Ebony called her "Kayda Bug." After hearing the term bug and Ebony mixing her name Kayda with it because she said, "She looks like a bug." Her nickname "Kayda-Bug!" stuck ever since!

Although Kayda has many nicknames: Kiwi, Baby Girl, Sugar Girl, and Baby Beast, Kayda-Bug is the name that has stuck the most. Kayda was such a sweet baby and she was a good sleeper. She did wake up every 2 to 4 hours to eat like most newborns, but after she ate, she would fall fast asleep. It was a matter of months before she started sitting up, smiling, and laughing. Kayda has always been a quick learner.

She was a very happy baby and she took her first steps at 9 months old and then walked unassisted at 10 months. Aunty Ebony was there the whole time helping me to care for her. Nikki had the baby touch and could always rock Kayda to sleep also. My mother would sing a bedtime song to her that I would sing to all of my children for bedtime when they were young. Kayda, now 12, used to sing the song for both her baby brothers and even made a special edition for Darren (her youngest brother).

Darren also has a few names he responds to like Kayda. He goes by Nathan, Baby, Chocolate Thunder, and D Money. Ayden, responds to Prince Abooboo (Ah-boo-boo), handsome, and Ayden Bayden. We can't forget Akira-Zoe, she's called Tiny Bot, Zoe, Akira, Tinky Wink, and Busy Bee. Even my dog has a few names Joi, Joy Joy, and Fluffy. I guess my family likes options!

Chapter Two - Kayda-Bug

Watching my baby walk was so cute because she was so small or short. She looked like a baby doll made alive. Many would ask, "How old is she?" I would tell them, and they were always surprised at her age because she was so small. I remember I had to go back to work after taking a year off to be home with Kayda-Bug.

I wasn't sure what I wanted to do, because it broke my heart to be away from her all day. I got so used to being with her all day and perhaps it was time I started to let her live a bit and get friends. I knew the day would come, but I just wanted more time with her. So I decided to slowly enter the workforce, taking a pay cut, by accepting a part-time job working with children. I decided to take a job offered by a great church to work in their toddler program.

I watched children ages 2 to 4 years old while their parents went to church service. I loved it so much, that I accepted a part-time three-day-a-week teacher position to teach my own class of 2-year-olds. The rule of the church, I could not teach in a class that had my child in it.

So I couldn't teach 1-year-olds, but sometimes I would see her passing by in the hallways when we had indoor playtime. We would have these cool buggy carts that could push 6 children at a time. She would be in the cart with her friends having a good time.

I realized she could handle being in class with a teacher and making friends. As I was finishing up my class, I started another part-time job working with an upholstery company on my off days. I would leave Kayda with a family friend's home daycare when I worked. Between the two classrooms, one day I noticed Kayda wouldn't put her foot all the way on the ground.

I was concerned about it and although she didn't cry when I touched her ankle or foot, she wouldn't walk on it. So the next morning I had called off my job to take her to her pediatrician. They took a look at her foot and wanted her to do an x-ray. It was pretty cool to wear the heavy jacket that repelled potentially harmful rays. It felt like a superhero suit! As she lay on the table and the nurse moved her foot and leg side to side to take pictures, Kayda-Bug didn't make a noise.

She was fascinated instead with the very bright light over her head. It felt like the sun lit up the room. It was so bright inside the room that my eyes had to adjust when we left out to the darker lighting in the next room we entered. We waited for the doctor to come and tell us what was going on.

The doctor entered several minutes after we waited. He came in full of energy and was a jolly man. He said, "Hi Kayda, I am Doctor Ken and I am going to tell you and your mom what happened to your ankle. Well, Mom, it looks like Kayda got a small fracture."

At the time I wasn't sure what the difference was between a fracture and a broken bone. I thought they were the same thing. Growing up, I never broke a bone or fractured one. I never even got a sprained ankle before.

So it was bizarre that a baby, barely a year old,

Chapter Two - Kayda-Bug

had a fractured ankle. A fracture is a crack in a bone and not a complete break. He showed me the X-ray images and pointed to the fracture. I asked the doctor, "Okay, so what happens next?"

He said, "Like with a broken bone, we would have to give her a cast." I thought, "Wow! A cast, for real, for a baby!" Yup, my little baby needed a cast and I thought I would need to schedule another appointment to get it done. Little did I know, a cast is like paper mâché. It is a cloth material that once wet hardens over time. Her cast was put on right in front of me by the doctor and within minutes he was all done!

My daughter didn't let her cast stop her from walking as I had feared. She would walk or run and it looked like she was swinging her foot to move it. Kind of like how you stir a spoon in an oval circular motion, she would swing her leg. Everyone was surprised at how quickly she could move with it on.

She didn't have to wear the cast long before it was cut off. I was happy when that day came, but her two legs looked very different. The one with the cast was skinnier and had a slight smell. It took what seemed like days and several baths for it to go away.

Her walk looked very different too after the cast came off. She still would walk and run with her leg stiff as a board even when she was cast free. We had to coach her into bending her knee and foot as she had done before at the start of walking. Within a month or so, she was back to normal.

CHAPTER THREE

The only thing was our lives were going to change. Before Kayda-Bug was 2 years old, I decided to move to Georgia. I needed a break from my life in Florida and a new state seemed like the best next step. Kayda was young when we moved and I remember like yesterday what it was like traveling with her. At this age, Kayda loved to sing. In the U-Haul we took from Florida to Georgia, it seemed like we sang the whole way there.

The time flew by because we were happily singing and driving together. Life was slightly less perfect than before, but we learned to take the good with the not-so-good. We moved in with my oldest brother Kelly

Chapter Three - Kayda-Bug

when we came to Georgia. I searched for a job and started working with a media agency. We worked with pastors who wanted to air their sermons on tv!

I did this for about a year and a half, and then I started my production company in Georgia. I have always enjoyed working for myself. I started my first production business in Florida when I was 18 years old. So this company was my second attempt to run a production business. I loved production and the first show I wrote and produced starred my niece Desiree. She would interview little people (children her age) and ask them questions. It was such a cute video and she did a great job!

When I started my business in Georgia I thought to launch an interview-based tv series entitled, "Total Restoration." I wanted to help business professionals connect their spiritual, professional, mental, and physical health goals to live an optimal life. To accomplish total well-being, I believe you have to strike a balance between the categories. On the show, I would interview experts in each space and ask them questions to draw out tips for their respective categories for watchers.

The show didn't catch on as a tv program at the time, so I thought about making it a radio program. It was beginning to catch on but I had too many expenses to keep it up. I decided to shift gears and stop production so I could focus on raising my daughter. I moved from writing programs to authoring and ghostwriting books instead.

I still have books in cue to publish. I plan to put out a book on the topic of Total Restoration, but I am not sure of when. Currently, I have published about 20 books, ghostwrote about 10 books, and edited 8 books for others so far. Perhaps in the next year, I will get that book done! My goal is to publish 50 books so I am about halfway there! My children are so proud of me.

Back to Kayda, that 2-year period seemed to go by quickly. Kayda-Bug grew quickly as any child does. One of my fondest moments was a song she would sing that she heard on the internet. The song was about whipping your hair around. My mother recorded Kayda's rendition of the music video on her phone. This video didn't look as good as the one she saw on tv–and her experience with the movie was very different. Every time we watch this video it sends us into laughter even still.

So the music is playing and Kayda-Bug is in it and singing along. She knows the lyrics for the most part, and she decides to get more into it. She starts swirling her head in a circle and moving her head back and forth. Her hair was moving as the song says, it was swaying a bit back and forth, but she did the move either too fast or too hard and something said, "Pop!" Kayda's eyes went super huge and she froze in place.

The noise made my mother's eyes instantly enlarge and she saw Kayda-Bug's energy die off completely, it sent her into instant laughter. Something to know about Kayda's grandma and my mom, she has a great sense of humor. That was one of her best gifts to her children and grandchildren, giving us a sense of humor.

Chapter Three - Kayda-Bug

After that pop, Kada-Bug didn't whip her neck again like that. She was more cautious and we all were after that. We leave the neck or extreme hair flip to the professionals.

My mom tried to encourage her to try it again after I examined her neck! Kayda-Bug learned her lesson and she didn't whip anything, only bobbed her head from side to side as she danced. She would rock her body but her neck was off-limits! Kayda was a fun and loving child. She loved to learn new things and she learned to spell many of her sight words quickly.

My only problem with Kayda was she would forget the words as quickly as she learned them. One week we would learn a set of words, then next week another set. The problem was when I did the review or mixed the words up from both weeks she would misspell a whole lot of them. I was growing frustrated because I felt like a failure.

I couldn't believe my degrees couldn't help me teach my own child English! I had a BA in English, minor credits in writing, was an author, got straight A's in many subjects, had a certificate for television production, and a master's in theology. Yet I felt like a total failure when she would mix up words. If that wasn't enough to make me feel sorry for myself, trying to teach her math made it worse. I quickly realized, that although I thought my education was sufficient to help me teach my daughter, I knew something had to be done differently.

She needed a teacher but I didn't want her to go to public school just yet. I wanted to control her environment so I decided to put her into a new startup school for girls. She went there for a few weeks but it wasn't working. Those two months seemed to push her further in the wrong direction. She was frustrated and I felt like I was running out of options.

I took a job waiting tables at the time because I burned out of working so hard for my company with little pay. Kayda-Bug and Akira-Zoe hung out with me and kept me busy. I used to only work about 4 nights a week to ensure I still had as much time as possible to take them to the park and such. I never wanted my work to take away their fun. I remember we used to go to an arcade regularly too.

This arcade is a known indoor playroom that our family had a few birthday parties over the years. I remember when Kayda-Bug turned 1 and she met her first human dressed in a short, but large-head mouse costume. She was okay when the character waved, but when it went to touch her, she burst into tears. Every time the mouse got close to her she would stare at it in fear.

I figured maybe she was just too young to appreciate characters at the time. Sad to say for the next five years she had the same anxiety towards not only that character but all of them! One year she was playing a game by herself. You see as she got older she stopped wanting to walk around the arcade with me and Zoe. She felt she was big enough to do her own thing, so she did.

Chapter Three - Kayda-Bug

One thing about this place, whenever the mouse was going to come out, music would always come on as a warning I learned over the years. When I heard the music I knew to go look for her. She was probably 4 years old at the time of this occurrence. She was so caught up in playing whack a mole, that she didn't even pay attention to the music. I mean she was handling her business and getting them all as I was watching from a few feet away.

It's funny because I was with her little sister, Tiny Bot at the time and she was just watching also. Zoe has always been a smart girl and she was good at watching Kayda make a fool of herself when a person in costume came out dancing. So the mouse came out and was doing his jolly dance and the fear that gripped Kayda's face was priceless! She instantly dropped the mallet and started scanning the room. I knew she was looking for me and I was certain if she didn't lock eyes with me soon she was going to burst into tears and start running.

We started making our way towards her and she saw us. The small tears that slid down her face dried up with a quickness as she latched onto my arm. I asked her, "Are you okay Kayda-bug?"

She replies, "Yeah, I'm good." Her words were calmer than her body language at the time. I gave her a good squeeze and we went to the opposite side of the arcade. I asked her, "Do you want to go dance with the kids?" She quickly responds, "No."

"Do you want to go pick up some free tickets? You know they are going to start throwing them out soon?'

"No, I'm good." She watched the other kids dance with the large mouse and Akira-Zoe was with that group. She couldn't help but dance and grab the tickets as they were tossed about by the mouse and helpers. I told Kayda, "You know it is okay to be afraid or nervous, but you don't want to miss out on enjoying life because of fear. You will find that under the suit and large head, likely a woman my size is in there. I'm not so scary am I?"

"No, but I know you. And what type of person would want to put that on?"

"A person who wants a job. You gotta relax," I told her, "and enjoy being a kid." Kayda was always asking some of the craziest questions. She started giving advice when she turned 2 years old. She was fast to pick up speaking and many were shocked that she communicated so well.

Kayda-Bug has always been cautious though. She was the type of child who would put her toe in the water before jumping into the pool. Kayda is okay with taking small steps. She was never game about taking unnecessary risks. I remember at the playground she would always take the stairs. There would be monkey bars to get across. A cylinder that spun when you put your foot on it. Even with soft tire mulch underneath, she didn't want to fall, so she would stand on the ground and spin the cylinder instead!

Chapter Three - Kayda-Bug

I would try to get her to be brave and jump, but she never did until she was ready. Zoe would be walking across bars, jumping off swings, or swinging from monkey bars, but not Kayda. She would watch and see people's results. I believe there is value in studying others and seeing what happens. You just don't want to do so much watching that you never live!

I remember the first time Kayda took a risk and walked these rings to get to the top of a playground set. I was so surprised and proud of her; Zoe was too. We both cheered her on but she wouldn't let us push her forward. At the time we were watching these competitive shows for people who enjoyed obstacle courses.

Man, sometimes it was funny to see people fall in the water because they slipped or missed a bar. We even went to some indoor playrooms to live the experience ourselves, and wow it was fun! It was so hard to pull your body weight during certain exercises though. But those shows and seeing Zoe do things encouraged Kayda to try some things herself. Sometimes life is that way, we need to watch others to build up our confidence. Don't be ashamed if you do that too!

After this, I realized she could use more social interaction with others. I know she loves her baby sister but they are 5 years different and on two different waves of life. I don't want her to feel as if she is missing out on life. I have never had a huge issue with growing up in public schools. To be honest, it was the only type of education I knew.

It wasn't until I became an adult that I saw some

differences in children with other experiences. I saw that some mothers homeschooled their children in their younger years and I thought of doing the same. Only to realize I wasn't the best and she needed something more than I could give. Not just with my teaching ability, but her desire to make friends.

Kayda when she was younger was an open book. You could tell her anything and she had so much confidence it wouldn't matter. You could laugh at her doing something silly and she would enjoy it. I remember when she was about three years old and singing into a brush!

She was at home with her grandma and my mother. Her hair had just been unbraided and she was trying to get a break. My mom tends to do things like hair while playing the tv or music to help occupy the time. This time it was gospel music.

We were all in love with this young talent from Brazil who would sing a song with the lyrics, "worthy is the lamb" and Kayda loved it! The boy's voice was so amazing because he couldn't be older than 9, but he had a low manly growl that he could pull out that was super cute! I always wanted to have young boys that could sing because of him.

On that day, Kayda had just gotten so excited she took the brush and stood up. She looked at my mom and said "Working is the lamb, working is the lamb!" My mom and I thought it was so cute! Her singing into that brush like it was a microphone had us so tickled. Not because she looked a bit wild with her hair, but also

Chapter Three - Kayda-Bug
because she had the words all wrong.

My mom and I giggle even to this day about how she sang "working is the lamb" instead of 'worthy is the lamb.' Kayda's grandmother loved encouraging her as she kept singing with confidence by saying, "Sing it baby! Working is the lamb!" We enjoyed her so much, we took like an hour's break to let Kayda-Bug give us a concert! That brush was on fire and she grew tired of singing and dancing after a long while had passed.

When the brush dropped at her completion, my mom finished her hair as she slept soundly in her lap. Kayda always is precious to me when I see her at rest… sleeping. It is when she is sleeping that I can really see how much she has grown. It is crazy how little babies are 19 inches, 6.1 pounds, and then they grow up to be several feet tall! Kayda is almost my height at 12, and she thinks she can take me at wrestling. I had to put her in a surprising headlock just to remind her "I am still boss!" Man it was funny to see her get hemmed up!

CHAPTER FOUR

She thought to wrestle me one day, and I did a beautiful maneuver that landed her in a headlock. She tapped out in laughter and asked me, "Hey where did you learn that? Teach me!" I jokingly replied, "See, momma, got a few tricks up her sleeve still. I can still take you out. Don't think because you are almost taller than me, I am still not Mommy."

My older siblings always got a kick out of my children calling me mommy. My sons float between mama and ma, as does Zoe too. I guess it is because my last three children are my country-speaking babies. The three of them were born in Georgia whereas Kayda was

Chapter Four - Kayda-Bug

born in Florida. I was born in Illinois but my mother is from Indiana. She has a country twang that comes out heavy from time to time. Mine is hit and miss but I love putting on a Southern Belle accent when I can for fun!

Other times I am just as country as my grandfather. One of the traits that stayed with Kayda for a long time in her younger years was sucking on those two fingers. Everywhere she went and without thinking the two fingers would rest in her mouth. I remember we tried everything to get her to stop. My mom told me to put lemon juice on them.

She made a sour face and drank the lemon juice. She took a licking but kept on ticking! Then my grandfather said, "Put some hot sauce on there!" My grandfather is a very countryman who loves spicy peppers. Every country he seems to love! Hunting, fishing, cooking, talking, and his voice is so cool because it is country too!

I can sit for hours and listen to him tell jokes with his distinguished way of telling stories. I told him, "I can't put hot sauce on there." He replied jokingly, "If you want her to stop you will." My grandfather was also an avid gardener. He loved to grow his own peppers and veggies right in his front yard. I enjoyed seeing his large grin as he brought something in from outside to cut up and add to his pot!

He and my grandmother are great cooks! I remember when I brought Kayda-Bug to Indianapolis to meet them. She was about a year old at the time and she was quiet. My grandmother told me, "Oh you can leave her with us anytime. She is so quiet." Kayda has always been a bit shy around new people, but when she is comfortable she isn't so shy.

Of the several pictures we took in Indiana to catch her in group photos, a few she had her fingers in her mouth. One thing about grandma and cooking, she will feed you. Kayda tried so many different foods and today my grandfather still cooks for a mini basketball team all these years later. Kayda-Bug will always give his menu a try.

My grandfather loves a person who will try his food or specialty drinks. He makes my children root-beer floats with vanilla ice cream. He made one once with ginger al and ice cream. It too was very tasty. I would admit, I never learned to cook quite like my granddad, but I sure love to eat mostly everything he cooks. The only thing I am not the biggest fan of is fish.

I never was a seafood eater growing up. I think it was because my mom is allergic so she never cooked it either. My grandfather, on the other hand, would cook fish every few days. He knew the names of the many fish he cooked and he had me try many of them. I liked to eat two of them, flounder and haddock. He can make fish not taste fishy, I know, strange, but true. The only fish I ate before his cooking was salmon.

My mom would make us salmon croquettes that we all loved. She would take ground-up salmon, made like tuna, and put it with eggs and crackers. She would mix the ingredients in a bowl and season them before molding them into patties. Three at a time she would put them into the skillet. She would let them brown up

Chapter Four - Kayda-Bug

nicely to where they were firm, but not burnt or extra crispy.

I loved how it would become crispy on the outside and soft on the inside. She would always serve hers with spaghetti. I liked eating them with or without noodles. I can eat them by themselves as a meal too. Funny I don't care for crabcakes, but I love salmon croquettes!

Kayda was a fan of croquettes too and would compare grandma's to her great-grandfather's. I am not sure who won but whoever was eating surely was a winner. Have you ever heard of the phrase, "winner, winner, chicken dinner?" I used to always think it was hilarious to hear.

So yeah, I didn't do the hot sauce thing to try to get her to stop sucking on her fingers. I believe Kayda-Bug was almost 5 before she gave up the fingers. I remember it was summertime and she went to Florida to be with her dad. Each year she spent the summer with her father and it was always a fun time for her.

She went there this year and her dad asked me about it. "Hey, do you think she is getting too old to still suck on her fingers?" I told him, "Yeah, I think it is time for her to give it up. But I have tried everything. I even painted her nails and told her if she sucks her fingers I wouldn't polish them anymore. But nothing is working."

Kayda always wanted her nails done. But I knew she would put her fingers in her mouth, so I wouldn't paint them. I thought her desire to get her nails painted would motivate her to ditch the two fingers. It didn't, within hours the polish was chipping and coming off. I quickly took it off to prevent her from getting poisoned by the chemicals in the polish.

I tried money, snacks, and going places if she stopped for a week–didn't work. I told him, "Good luck and you have my blessings and prayers!" To this day I am still not sure the trick or logic he used to get her to stop, but she did! Kayda-Bug has always been fond of her father. She wants so much to impress him. I guess all children have that inner feeling to want to please someone.

Although I wished she didn't want to impress the wrong people, I can't say that didn't become the case. When Kayda was 5, this was when she wanted to impress her cousins. She loved them so much! One was 5 years older than her, Syeda and the other was 10 years her senior, Desiree. The girls were different from Kayda and they pointed out those differences. The problem with anyone showing you how you differ from them is when it makes you not like yourself.

Kayda was the fondest of Syeda. She loved her hair, how skinny she was, and that she was cool in her eyes. It pained me to hear them call Kayda fat or when she got the nickname Baby Beast. It really made her start looking at herself differently and she still battles with body image and self-love. Although nicknames may be intended to be funny, they still can create insecurities in a person.

It was at this time, more than ever, that Kayda started questioning her beauty. She would ask me, "Is

Chapter Four - Kayda-Bug

my hair pretty mommy?"

I would respond, "You have gorgeous hair. I like your hair more than mine sometimes. It is thick, long, and can keep twist very well."

"Yeah, but I wished my hair was long like Syeda's," she replied.

"I told her, "Your hair is longer than mine it is just curly." Her hair would shrink when it was not pressed. She had the cutest puffs growing up, but after seeing her cousin's hair she wanted straight flowing hair.

Syeda's hair was silky when pressed, so she wanted her hair pressed. I was never good at doing hair. Although I could crochet, sew, and knit, I didn't know how to braid! Can you imagine having two girls with the perfect hair type to braid, and not knowing a lick of how to do it? I mean my fingers felt uncomfortable, they would cramp up from holding them in a weird position. So the best I could do was ponytails.

I wasn't the greatest at making parts or separating the hair into even sections at all. It seemed my parts were always crooked no matter how hard I tried. So I stopped trying to get them straight! I made some bigger than others on purpose and the style came out much better. Sometimes we have to embrace our flaws to appreciate our differences. My daughter loved them in the beginning, but now she is desiring something else.

Sometimes when we outgrow what someone else loves, it can be difficult. This wasn't the first time this had happened with Kayda-Bug and me. In fact, I know it won't be the last time either. She tried to fit in with her cousin and even with their compliments, at times it wasn't enough. Have you ever been happy about something and then you see what someone else has or thinks, you become less interested in that thing? Her hair was cute but it was not the same as Syeda's.

Her hair texture is beautiful to me. It can be in puffs, an afro, braids, or even pressed to a soft and flowy–or slightly frizzy straight look. She is so versatile and her hair to this day is longer than mine. The only problem with getting these styles is the time or pain it takes to make it happen. Loose braids don't wear the same or as long as tighter ones. To get straight flowy hair you have to blow dry and use a flat iron.

For frizzy straight, you only have to blow dry, and you need to wash and then blow-dry to get the best braids. It is a process and Kayda always hated any pain associated with her hair. We call that tender-headed from where I am from. Others may say she's sensitive, no matter what you call it she is that. I would take my time doing her hair, add water, put her ponytails loose, and all to no avail.

She would cry the entire time and I mean the ugly kind of cry. You know when you don't care what you look like, snot can be running, tears rolling, and you start doing a self-inflicted shake with the anticipation of the comb coming back around. I remember at times I wasn't doing anything, just holding her hair in my hand, and she would wince and raise her shoulders. If I thought to bring the comb closer, she would start

Chapter Four - Kayda-Bug

complaining before I did one comb-through.

I was like, "I am not going through 18 years of this!" We are going to find a style that lasts, is painless, and I can manage with my limited means and skill. That was when my twist game was brought into action! I would twist her hair into individual braids and it would last about a week or two.
We loved our twist.

Kayda has gorgeous thick hair like me. It grows very fast and to do her hair would take at least 2 hours. Tiny Bot's hair is thinner so it didn't take but an hour or less! I finished her hair so quickly that I would add beads because I wasn't tired. They both loved to add beads. The last time I beaded Kayda's hair it took about 20 beads to cover half the braid. Now, a 2-hour style would take an extra 30 minutes.

But these styles grew less and less desirable as Kayda got older. Using a flat iron was never my thing neither was using a curling iron. I remember one time when I was about 11 years old I wanted to have a bang.

I got my mom one day to cut it for me but the roller she put in to make the curl didn't do much. My hair again is very thick so that roller was busting with hair like uncooked dough bursting out of a slightly popped canister. It was funny to look at the roller sit-up weird off my forehead. When my hair dried, my curl was floppy and didn't hang right at all.

I thought, "I can fix this." I always saw my older sister, Nikki, doing her hair in the mirror. Maybe I could do the same thing? Wrong! I plugged the curling iron in and watched it get hot! I was excited to see the red button. Finally, it looks hot enough after about 30 seconds or a minute of waiting. I combed my piece of hair and I examined the iron before I started. I saw where the black ring was to place my fingers as I curled.

I picked it up after a quick silent prayer. Pushed the lever down to open the claw and stuck my hair in between the plate. A strange smell quickly filled the room and I heard sizzling. I got scared and thought let me hurry up and spin it. You have to turn the curling iron several times to wrap the hair around. The only problem I was looking at the counter and not the mirror because I was afraid to burn my eyelashes!

I mean I saw the smoke and felt the heat. I tried to spin it and hold the black piece at the end. But I missed it and burned my hand. I panicked and let the curling iron go and it rolled down my cheek but was still holding onto my hair! I quickly grabbed the handle and pressed the lever, I had a curly but also a red mark on my face for where I was lightly seared.

Chapter Four - Kayda-Bug

CHAPTER FIVE

Man, I never got over that anxiety. Even as I got older and would get my hair pressed, feeling the heat would make me flinch, bring up my shoulders, close one of my eyes really tight, and do the ugly face. This face is when you stretch your cheeks and your smile looks as if someone outstretched it as far left and right as your mouth can go.

I was embarrassed I burned myself and I stayed away from irons long after that. I didn't even want much to do with ironing my clothes! Too many times I went to school wrinkled because I was afraid to burn myself.

Chapter Five - Kayda-Bug

I have burned myself a few times with a clothing iron and I dropped it once on the floor!

So I know the cautious part of Kayda or the fearful part could have had something to do with me. After I see something fail, I am not the type of person to be gung-ho about doing it again. I watch, study, and try to learn vicariously whenever I can. Kayda-Bug is the same way.

We both have to learn to live a little and be okay with being less than perfect. This is easier said than done, I know. Who really wants to fail anyway? Failure is a part of life but you don't want that to be a revolving theme. I must tell you, I tried to improve Kayda and Zoe's adventurous side. I didn't want them to be afraid to try new things because they might not be good at it on their first attempt.

I remember when Kayda thought of joining a dance class. It was something her father and I supported. When she told me her dad had enrolled her I was happily impressed and surprised. I felt it would give her time to bond with girls her age. She was about 6 or 7 at the time. She wanted me to take her to the first class because her dad wasn't able to do it.

So we get dressed and head to the studio. This dance class was a hip-hop or group dance class. Nothing super serious like ballet, jazz, or something like that. The girls were all dressed in regular clothes so I was glad I didn't go over the top with putting her in a dancer outfit.

I took my seat to watch because when I looked like I was going to leave, Kayda's eyes got big and I knew that meant to sit down. As the girls were encouraged to come on the floor by the instructor I looked on like the few other moms trapped into staying. Not that I was unhappy to be there, I just saw this class as a way for me to get some time to clean and get things done at home.

The girls line up and the instructor tells them, "Alright I am going to turn on the music but we are going to warm up first. I want you to keep your eyes on me and don't worry if you mess up." She presses play and the music starts. I can't say I was familiar with the song, at the time I only knew gospel songs and that is mostly still all I listen to and oldies music. I stopped listening to mainstream music around the time I was 19 years old. At this time, I was about 29.

The teacher begins with what looks like a march and she brings her arms up. She then does a few more steps ranging from going side to side and kicking. I might point out, that although I was in training to be a dance mom, I was a dancer growing up. I did every dance I could: hip-hop, Caribbean, salsa, Latin dances, ballroom, and even country-line dancing. I have always loved to dance.

Being here brought back memories and it was cute to see Kayda struggle to follow the steps and keep up with the teacher. She was clearly growing a bit impatient. As she tried to keep her spirits up, she would look toward me and her sister Zoe who came with us. We both would smile and encourage her to keep going. She turned back to the teacher and kept trying to quicken or slow her feet down.

She looked like she could be shifting from discomfort to fun, but suddenly the teacher had the girls

Chapter Five - Kayda-Bug

lift their arms out to their sides. Kayda was a bit closer to the girl next to her than when she started. The footwork had her traveling. The girl next to her, without noticing her travels, throws her arms up and out and slaps Kayda in the face!

Zoe and I tried to hide our faces because we saw the ordeal, we tucked our heads low and started to laugh. We couldn't hold it in and we saw Kayda's reaction to the slap which made us laugh all the more. She backed away from the line when she got slapped. She threw her hands up and got so frustrated, that she started stomping her feet off the floor in our direction.

I tried to compose myself and assure Kayda it was an accident when she told me, "Mommy, did you see that girl just slap in my face?"

I held my laughter and tried to have a straight face, "Yes honey, I saw it. But she didn't do it on purpose. She was just dancing and you were too close. It's okay. You're okay." I checked her face to where she could see and be assured she was fine. "You are not bleeding or anything. Just go have fun."

She replied, "I don't want to dance no more."

I looked her in the eyes, "Aww Kayda-Bug it's okay. You want to just sit down and see if you want to get back up and dance with the girls?" She nodded and sat down next to me. We three sat together and watched the girls twirl around and have fun. I told Kayda when the class was over, "See, that wasn't so bad. You can do this!"

"It wasn't bad for you, you didn't get slapped in the face!" She was giggling about it now, but I could tell she was serious and likely wouldn't be back. I had to call the instructor and her dad to let them know she didn't want to come back. Since then, Kayda-Bug makes sure she has plenty of room when she dances between her and the next person. She will gently push someone before she lets them get too close to her too!

I know sometimes our experiences can make us want to run away from trying something again. I like that Kayda-Bug didn't give up on dancing, she just became wiser. She knows now the importance of keeping her position and helping others to stay in their places when they dance too.

I remember recently when Kayda was 11, her grandma and I were teaching her several partnered dance steps. She loves to two-step, a famous dance style from Chicago, and slow dance. I am sure she is going to invite her dad to teach her some moves also.

She enjoys playing video games that include teaching dance moves too. Zoe and her even try to get me involved. I am not a big gamer but I get how others can like them and spend hours playing. Something else Kayda loves is school. Ever since I brought her to her first homeschool, she has been hooked on this kind of learning environment.

The initial school was a bit tough as I mentioned earlier. The instructor couldn't spend a whole lot of time with one student. She had 4 different grade levels in one

Chapter Five - Kayda-Bug

classroom. My daughter at the time was the youngest and she didn't have the basics down.

She was struggling in math and reading at the time. She desired to be a good student, and I supported it, but it was not happening. I realized the environment was not one in which she could learn best. She was too young to read a book or instructions and know what to do by herself. She still needed a teacher who could walk her through the steps.

When I pulled her out of that school I was nervous. I didn't have a huge budget to put her in a private school and I didn't have the skill or patience to teach her myself. I was running my own business then as I am doing now, and the time she needed I couldn't give. If I have to choose between being a good mom and a good teacher for her, I will always choose to be a great mommy!

So I remember getting my hair down–as a gift from a friend. I talked to her about my problem and she mentioned this lady named Mrs. Beverly. I couldn't wait to meet her. I wanted to learn about her school and meet her in person. My hairstylist told me nothing but great things and I was excited. Mrs. Beverly was a retired teacher. She is an expert in peeping (seeing) games students like to play. She can tell a mile away if a child is sincere or coming up with a cunning story to get over.

She is not shy about calling out foolishness when a student tries to turn in subpar work. When I came to visit the first time, I felt her grandma vibe and I loved it. It was what my daughter needed! The first month

Kayda-Bug was in her class her reading had improved so much I wanted her sister to join!

At the time Zoe was almost fully potty trained and that was the requirement. They could come if they were potty trained. I got her there in a month and she was 3 years old learning with Mrs. Beverly too! Within 6 months they were both readers! Akira today can read on a 5th-grade level in 3rd grade. Kayda can read on an 8th-grade level in 6 grade.

These two girls were always smart, but seeing them advance so quickly assured me I made the right decision to go this route over public school. I was talking to a sister of mine, she is like my older sister because we are such close friends. TC was talking to me about a paper she was reviewing and how she personally felt the public school system failed her.

She said it wasn't until she got to college she realized she never learned the basics of the English language. She didn't know how many sentences were in a paragraph, the reasons for the use of a comma, and why having a word twice in a sentence wasn't good for academic writing. Starting a sentence with "and" or "but" was also a problem she discovered in college and not high school!

Some schools poorly prepare even the smartest people, because TC has gone on to obtain her doctorate. She is a wonderful licensed counselor, and super smart in finance, and banking. If I ever need someone to read over my books or give an honest opinion of content flow, I always tap her shoulder.

Chapter Five - Kayda-Bug

I was so impressed by what she accomplished with them in such a short time. We love her so much, 5 years later they are still with her. That's what you do with good people, you always stay connected because you appreciate them. All the moments were great with academics, it has not been roses every day.

Kayda-Bug is a great student. She enjoys getting her work done and when she completes her work she is looking for what she can do to stay ahead. She enjoys free days, so she will work hard now to rest on the weekend. Mrs. Beverly would have to tell her to stop working at lunch and rest because she was so deadset on getting her work done.

CHAPTER SIX

I guess that is also something I struggle with too! It's hard for me to start something and not finish it. Kayda has always been a great student, but she struggles with getting along with others or making new friends and school highlighted that. Mrs. Beverly is always polite when it comes to correction. She will pull a parent to the side and give them the rundown so they know what happened and what she did to correct the situation.

Kayda-Bug got teased by a particular student often. Yes, a form of bullying is in every school no matter how small it would seem. Her class had about 15 students in it, but the school was about 20 to 30 children

Chapter Six - Kayda-Bug

at a time. Mrs. Beverly and her sister, Mrs. Mya, run the school together. I am so grateful for Mrs. Mya too. I think it is great the two of them can work together and support each other's dreams. She too is an educator with a no-nonsense radar.

This particular girl would push Kayda's books on the floor. Make fun of her clothes, shoes, and hair; really, everything about her. Kayda wasn't a heavy girl, but she was also not skinny at this time, she was just solid. She would pick on her to the point she would feel like she had to defend herself or win this girl's approval so others would be her friend. This girl once told her for them to be friends, Kayda-Bug would have to give her, her necklace.

Desiring to be friends and squash whatever beef they had she gave the girl the necklace. The girl was planning to keep it and still not be friends with Kayda. My daughter didn't understand, that you don't pay for friendships. Good relationships are built on lasting interest and mutual desire to be friends. Anyone that makes you feel that you have to buy them things, or give them things for them to pay attention to you, doesn't truly know your worth I had to tell her.

True friends like you for you first. It is not about what they can get, but how you make them feel when they are around you. Also, good friends want to build you up even if telling you a harsh truth is necessary. After telling you something difficult they won't leave you or try to hurt you in the process either. Learning your value is critical because you will constantly meet people who will tell you that you don't matter. Don't believe them!

This conversation started when she was about 6 and at 12 we are still rehashing this conversation. We have to revisit it because until she believes it, she settles for the wrong ideas about herself. There are people in the world that will compare their beauty, weight, grades, parent's success, where they live, or what they have in comparison with others. The message to those with a lot or a little is the same, you gotta love yourself!

I told Kayda, "People bully others because they lack confidence or validation in themselves. Oftentimes, people don't wake up in the morning and say I want to be a bully. They are groomed into one." It can be so hard for me to have conversations with Kayda-Bug that I know hurt her feelings. Who wants to hear, "This person doesn't like you now and they may not like you later either. Never compromise yourself just to please others. You will learn they will use you and you could grow to hate yourself."

Have you ever made changes to please someone else and found out, "Wow, I don't like doing this or looking like that. I tried it, but this isn't me?" I have too many times, especially when I was young, of changing myself to be accepted only to reject myself. I had to learn to love myself with the gaps in my teeth. At the time, my braids and not straight hair. Being short and not tall. Or skinny and not thick.

We all wanted to be accepted and Kayda wanted this girl to like her until she realized the girl never would. She started disregarding the comments she

Chapter Six - Kayda-Bug

made to her. Kayda-Bug quit giving her things or going out of her way to be friends with her. Then boom! She wanted to be friends with Kayda now. The friendship didn't last long and it hurt her feelings some when she found out the girl had a party and didn't invite her.

I told her, acquaintances are cool too! These are people you speak to when you see them. You two may even have a great time, but at the end of the day, you both are not that close when you go home. The two of them never had phone conversations or hung out outside of class. Also, all children don't have the same idea of friendship as others. Cultural and household differences can change how people see the same thing.

I was so very proud of Kayda-Bug that year. When this girl left the school it was a day she celebrated. I was happy that she was at peace and she made friends that year. There were also things Kayda noticed going to school that were different from our home. She couldn't watch the same videos or listen to the same music as some of her friends. I remember they got technology time a few days out of the week. One of the girls was watching something on YouTube that showed kissing, and Kayda said, "I can't watch this!"

She went and sat by herself in class and Mrs. Beverly inquired why she was sitting alone. She told Mrs. Beverly what the other students were watching, and her teacher banned YouTube watching unless it was school-oriented during technology time. I think she made some "frienemies" (people who pretend to be friends but are enemies) that day. Kayda is truthful to a fault at times. I would not say she hasn't lied or doesn't get caught in a lie now and again. For the most part, especially in school, she is the truthful one.

Sometimes being truthful can equate to being compared to a tattletale. My youngest Zoe tends to overshare information not requested. I remember once even Mrs. Beverly said, "I don't think you should share that" when Akira ran up to her to give a report. I think it had something to do with which student had let out a loud fart!

Mothers may talk as if their children are perfect, but every mother knows better than to believe that! So what was something Kayda-Bug did that threw me for a loop? I remember she was in 3rd or 4th grade. Again at this time, she was still going to school in person and not online. The last two years have been online since the Covid outbreak, I will talk more about that in a few. Funny how Covid rushed the process to be a few months sooner.

Back to the case in point, Kayda has always wanted to express herself in clothing. I guess this is a right of passage for everybody. My toddlers think they know what they want to wear too. Don't even talk about food. My youngest Nathan is quick to gently push your hand away and shake his head no.

He even voices the word no and will dance his index finger from left to right when he says it. Too grown! This child has had social cues down pack starting around 3 months. He was walking at 9 months and holding his head up at 2 months. Not sure what COVID did to this generation, but they are sharp!

Chapter Six - Kayda-Bug

Now with my Kayda-Bug, she decided to alter her attire at school. I guess she felt her outfit was either outdated or made her hot, I really wasn't sure what it was. I can tell you this. She went to school with a pair of jeans on, a cute shirt, and a blue vest. The vest of course had no sleeves but a cute silver zipper in the front. The outfit was layered in such a cute way.

I guess the outfit wasn't a skirt like she had wanted to wear on this day, so she thought to modify her attire using what she had. Most girls take an extra bag of clothes to school and change there, but Kayda didn't do that. So she went into the bathroom with jeans on and came out with a skirt. Only, it wasn't a skirt. Kayda was resourceful and thought to take her vest off and morph it into a skirt.

She made this versatile vest skirt by sliding the vest down past her stomach and zipping it up! I guess she wanted a zip-up skirt! I would have admitted it could have been a great cheat for a YouTuber, only there was a problem. When she went to sit down the skirt vest malfunctioned.

The vest zipper dipped down as she sat in her chair. She had a lot of eyes on the skirt because no one had seen her wear one. I didn't care too much for them, not for any reason, we just normally bought jeans, shorts, or dresses. She quickly got compliments for being fashionable and she loved the attention. The commotion in the room had Mrs. Beverly do a double-take and she asked Kayda to stand up again.

Only this time she couldn't. She instantly burst into tears and her teacher came to her side. "What's wrong? You okay? I just wanted to see your skirt?"

"No, I can't stand up," Kayda cried out as tears rolled down her face. Her back is hunched over and she hovers over to Mrs. Beverly. Her teacher guides her out of the class to spare her some emotional backlash, although some of the work has already been done. As they step slightly outside the classroom, Mrs. Maya steps into the class on behalf of Mrs. Beverly. The two walk down the hall for Mrs. Beverly to better understand the situation.

"Okay Kayda, now tell me what is going on? Why can't you stand?"

"It hurts," she swoons in pain. Her tears get heavier and her voice carries in the hallway.

"Okay, Kayda-Bug you are going to have to calm down so I can understand you. What is stuck?"

Chapter Six - Kayda-Bug

CHAPTER SEVEN

Kayda lifted her shirt that was overlapping the zipper. The zipper had shimmed down a patch of her skin and now it was stuck! Mrs. Beverly looks at it and says, "Oh baby, wow that doesn't look good at all. We are going to have to call your mom."

Kayda hollers out, "Noooo! Please, please don't call my mom!" She shakes her head from left to right and starts drying her tears. It was as if cold water was tossed in her direction.

"Now you know I have to. Why would you do this to yourself?"

Chapter Seven - Kayda-Bug

"I just wanted a skirt. Can we not call my mom, can you just try to help me? I will be okay. It's starting to hurt less already anyway."

"Kayda you cannot leave your skin sandwiched inside that zipper."

"But if my mom comes up here I am going to be in big trouble."

"I would say your skin is already in trouble. Let me call your mom and whatever you do, don't sit down."

Meanwhile, I am working at my upstairs office across the street and two blocks down the road. I frequently walked to their school to eat lunch with them from time to time. Or if the weather was permitting, I would walk to pick them up to get out and breathe some fresh air. I love walking. It is one of my favorite pastimes besides playing tennis.

My phone rings and it is Mrs. Beverly, I remember thinking, 'Hmmm, I wonder why she is calling? It was past lunch but before school releases.' I answered the phone and she said, "Hi Kayda's mom," not in a chipper way like normal, but in an inquisitive way that made my mommy radar click on. "Hey, Mrs. Beverly. Did something happen, everything alright?"

"Do you mind coming to the school? Are you close?"

"Yeah, I am at my office. Is Kayda or Akira having a problem?"

"Well, Kayda has a situation. But I think it is best if you come down and see."

"Okay, I am on my way." I took my cell phone and tucked it into my pocket. I put markers on the work I was doing and made sure to turn off my coffee pot. I don't drink coffee, but I love hot tea. I can even drink it without sugar. My children think it is nasty without it, but I love it with a squeeze of lemon, honey, and cayenne pepper from time to time. After turning that off, I turn my sign around, turn off the lights, and lock the door.

I jog down the stairs and out the main door. I am enjoying the summer sun and gentle breeze as I walk. The walk almost made me forget why I had to leave my office in the first place. I arrived at the Mexican restaurant on the corner and I realized how hungry I was. It is strange how I can get so enamored with working I forget to eat! Now I am starving.

I walked across the street when it was safe to travel and walked up to the office plaza where the school was located. I knock on BeTutored's door and appears Mrs. Beverly with a lingering smile. "Thanks for coming and sorry to pull you away from your office."

"It's alright. I told you if you ever need me, just let me know."

"You know your daughter told me not to call you."

I do a dry chuckle, "She must have done some-

Chapter Seven - Kayda-Bug

thing pretty drastic for you to call." Mrs. Beverly signals for Kayda to come up towards the front. I see Kayda come through the door hunched over but what I don't see is her pants!

I instantly ask, "Kayda, what happened to your pants? Don't tell me you peed on yourself. Oh no, you didn't start your–"

"No mom…" She says in a low grumbled voice.
"Why are you standing like that? Stand up straight, and lift up your head girl." I came closer to her and she quickly responded, "I can't Mom."

"Wait a minute, are you wearing your vest as a skirt?" Unable to contain my laughter, I chuckle out of peer shock. After I quickly collect myself, I say, "Come on we have to go to the bathroom and get this fixed."

The two of us shuffled into the bathroom and Kayda-Bug up until now has been very composed. I said, "Okay let me see it. Maybe it isn't as bad as you think." Kayda lifted her shirt and I saw her skin zip into the zipper. It looked like a crinkled baby sausage busting out of a can!

It looked very painful and I surely didn't want to have to touch it. If I looked like I was going to tap it, she would wince in pain. I knew this wasn't going to work to try and talk her through unzipping it. She would panic and the control she had was out of the window. Her hands were at her sides doing a praise dance shake as I looked at the situation. I knew we would have to take this surgery on the road.

If anyone could do what needed to be done, it was Grandma! I went and grabbed the car, left work early that day, and headed to my mother. My mom had been doing this mothering thing longer than me. She has seen all kinds of challenges and she was prepared for this I was sure.

I don't doubt for a second a good laugh will come out of this. Yes, the apple did not fall far from the tree there! When my daughter came into the house hunched over and walking like a 90-year-old woman, my mom sprang into action.

She said, "Kayda-Bug I hear you are having some issues with your skirt?"

"Yeah, I kinda got my skin caught."

"Yeah, your mom told me. So let's go to the room so I can see what you've done to yourself," replies my mother. The two of them walk together toward her room with Tinki Wink and I following behind them. We get into the room and Kayda takes off her jacket exposing the pain she inflicted on herself.

Without the slightest hesitation, Grandma says, "Girrlll, now how you do this?" That girl was the longest pronunciation of the word I've ever heard and it was followed by roaring laughter as she finished her sentence. My mom had tears in her eyes for a few moments because she just couldn't believe it.

She says, "Wow! This is the stuff that happens to

Chapter Seven - Kayda-Bug

God's children when they do stupid stuff. This right here should have never happened. Do you think this was a good idea?"

My mother never skips a moment to teach anyone a life lesson. She isn't lying though. Many times I have done silly things and was instantly corrected by God (Yah). I mean I would be complaining about something in the kitchen, and bam! Walk into a cabinet door.

Or I could be mumbling or saying something unproductive about myself, and wham! Bang my toe on the foot of the bed. It never fails for me to be instantly the recipient of correction when I deserve it. I see that the apple also didn't fall too far from the tree.

So now that my mother, Kayda's grandma has composed herself. She is ready to go into solution mode. She says, well the only way to get this off is to cut it off.

"What! Do you have to cut my vest? But I like my vest."

"Well, I am glad you liked it. But after I cut this piece off you will have a piece of it for memory sake and that is about it."

I responded, "Children always want more clothes. You buy them nice things and they turn them into tragedies. But honestly, I would have never thought you would do this. I thought you would have gotten a stain on it, ripped it in some mysterious way, or even cut it accidentally with scissors perhaps. This is completely original."

My mom and Kayda worked on getting the vest cut away. I was still thinking about how exactly was my mom going to get the zipper off being that her skin was crinkled up inside the ridges. I thought I was going to learn a thing or two about zippers that day.

I guess Kayda thought the process would change because the scissors were brought to the party. As the vest was cut away from Kayda's body the only part remaining was the zipper. I looked on without saying a word, and saw my mom quickly grab and seemingly yank the zipper down in a flash!

Kayda grabbed her stomach like she was sent into shooting pain. A bit of blood was present but it was quickly cleaned up. My mom disinfected the wound and Kayda was as good as new in a few moments. She admitted it was more painful with her skin in the zipper than several minutes after it was removed. The only way to still get a zipper off is to unzip it apparently. If it is not, don't tell Kayda. Lol!

Kayda that day learned a very crucial lesson about fashion, don't try to wear something that you cannot try on at the store and feel comfortable. Not everything one person wears will look good on you or make you feel comfortable. She wasn't shy to wear the skirt at first, but she told me when she got home she didn't like the attention or the exposure. S

he wanted to impress her friends, but she did that at a great expense to herself. I remember telling her,

Chapter Seven - Kayda-Bug

"You can impress people with clothes you like and that make you feel good. You can impress them with hairstyles you like, the way you talk, how smart you are, and so many other things. You don't have to become them to impress people who want to have you as their friend."

Kayda has always wanted to be a friend to others and to stick up for justice. I told her she would make a great school or class president someday because of that trait. I remember she told me about a boy in her class. I call him troublesome only because he seemed to get into a lot of trouble, not to mean he is in trouble everywhere he goes.

I pray at home and other places he was not. Maybe there were too many girls in his class? Maybe he liked girls in his class and that made him feel like he had to be different to get their attention. Many people struggle with getting others to see their uniqueness.

One day, he was minding his own business and walking back into the class to grab a few books from his shelf. He didn't see the chair slightly out in the walkway and his foot clipped the chair leg. Blam! His face planted onto the floor. Superhero Kayda-Bug was out to the rescue and she tried to help the young man get up from the floor and gather his books.

He did not like appearing weak before his peers. Instead of being grateful for the help, he came up off the floor swinging his book in front of Kayda's face. He missed her face but landed a book across her shoulder. She was shocked initially and the young man was reprimanded by their teacher

Kayda sustained no injuries but she should have learned a valuable lesson–especially with this young man, not everyone appreciates help. He wasn't grateful for her input on this day and one other occasion. Sometimes it takes two strikes or three for you to strike out.

With this kid, he struck out the second time. So the class was eating lunch as is customary each day. He normally struggled with his lunch but today it was vital that he ate so the class could get rewarded. Everyone in class saw that he was slow, so they were all encouraging him to eat.

Their teacher kept checking on them all to see their progress, and each time the result was the same, he simply wasn't eating–or at least not fast enough. Kayda-Bug finally thinks to rat him out because she wanted the cupcakes like everyone else. Another female classmate also told that he was not eating and can they just get the cupcakes.

The boy was so frustrated that they blasted him out, that he spun Kayda's chair around real fast in a circle and slapped the other girl on the back! The girl he slapped ended up wrestling with him as the teacher tried to break it up. You would have thought this was a big school or a troubled school because of some of the things that happened.

On another occasion, Kayda was talking to her class something she hardly ever does. A girl that wanted to pick on her that day, did not like that everyone was listening to Kayda and having fun so she decided to do

Chapter Seven - Kayda-Bug

something very strange. The entire time she was sitting in her seat she kept playing with something in her hands.

Kayda didn't think much about her silence or what she was playing with. The girl got up from her seat and walks over to her, she smiles at Kayda and moves to walk behind her. Kayda of course tries to keep her eyes on the girl as she moved, you can never take your eyes off someone who you know doesn't like you, who smiles at you then walks behind you. That is a no, no in school.

So as she tries to follow her almost straining her neck to follow, she feels several prickles hitting her skin and going down the front and back of her shirt. As she shook her shirt she discovered, the girl had dumped a box of loose staples over her head and shoulders. There were staples everywhere! Even when she came home that day I found a few in her hair.

CHAPTER EIGHT

I don't understand what makes people or children come up with such cruel plans to use against another person. Jealousy appears to be a very dangerous thing. If a person cannot appreciate or control your uniqueness, they tend to dislike you strongly for it. Sadly, some want to hurt you because they like something about you so much, that maybe they can't do it, so they want to change that about you. I am a big smiler. I smile all the time and can't help but laugh and be joyful.

I feel like at times people want to see what they can do to break my smile. Have you ever seen the British soldiers that stand guard at the palace? The many people who pass by it love to take pictures in front of

Chapter Eight - Kayda-Bug

the guards. Then there are those special cases, where taking a picture isn't enough.

Do they want to make the guard smile, laugh, or break character for some reason? I am not sure if these people feel it is a victory because it is a challenge to get the guards to break character. Maybe it makes them feel powerful in some kind of way.

I remember when I worked as a model when I was a teenager. We used to dress up in the clothes from the store and play manikin in the window. We would have to hold our poses for three minutes each and not move. I was super good at it. I never moved until it was time to change. Like the guards, I too, saw people coming by doing all kinds of things to make me laugh. Ironically, the woman that loves to smile and laugh, didn't break once. Many applauded because I didn't. It was a fun job while it lasted and it taught me how to stay focused no matter the distractions.

I would say this about Kayda-Bug, she has always been focused when it comes to food. There are all kinds of things she wanted to learn to make. She started with peanut butter and jelly sandwiches of course, but now she can do way more than that. I think it is amazing to look at her now sometimes when I remember where she came from. She used to be this small, short, tinny, walking, babydoll look-alike. Now she looks the same, walks, and talks, but she cooks too!

Kayda's first time in the kitchen was the use of a microwave. She knows how to make ramen noodles and can make them better than me with a microwave. I am not a fan of the machine at all. I prefer the stove or even a toaster oven over the microwave. I would always tell my children to use it as an extreme last resort. I am not too sure about the science of the side effects of the use of a microwave, but there is no reason to take a chance on radiation all to heat a pizza in 30 seconds! I will turn the stove or oven on and take a slow but sure approach any day!

I did have my concerns about Kayda using the microwave because her older cousin had some issues with the machine. We laugh about it now, but my sister wasn't happy about it when it happened. My second niece, Syeda, had a rough time with the microwave when she started using the kitchen. I am not sure what she thought to warm up, but the results were catastrophic! She and the stove became best friends.

So what did she do exactly? One time she set the machine to 30 minutes instead of 30 seconds, and the object she put into the microwave caught fire. The second time, she put a fork in the microwave! Everyone knows metal in a microwave is a no, no. It will start an electrical fire inside the box that would scare anyone. The machine started popping and smoking. The smell that filled the air smelled terrible. My sister quickly unplugged it and reminded her, "Do not put silverware in the microwave."

My older sister replaced the machine and in about another month, the same thing. A piece of silverware made it into the microwave and blew it up! So my sister banned her, and my grandma taught her how to cook with the stove. I do recall a time Kayda-Bug

Chapter Eight - Kayda-Bug

caused a fire! Guess where the fire started? The microwave!

So we went to our favorite restaurant for quick but tasty food. It may not be the healthiest because it is fried, but boy their service is exceptional! We cannot help but go and leave with a smile. I can at times get so excited that I order a bit more than what I think we can eat. Their food is so good though, I don't mind eating it sometime later when I warm it up. I normally don't eat leftovers, especially fried foods, but this sandwich is still good, and if in a pinch I can approve microwave use.

So Kayda-Bug decided to warm up her sandwich. The only problem, the wrapper had foil on the inside of the package. That sandwich caught fire so quickly. I said, "Kayda-Bug, Noo! We got to stop it." She saw the fire and moved back so I had to move swiftly and press the open button.

Mind you the fire is still going on the package. I taped the sandwich and put out the fire. The sandwich looked good still even with the ashes sprinkled around some of the edges. I said, "Hmmm, still looks mighty tasty." Kayda-Bug responded, "Aww mom, this sucks! I really wanted to eat it."

I said, "If you do, you better cut this half off and eat the rest. But if you won't I will take it, and give you mine." She took the chance to switch sandwiches and I did as I said. The sandwich tasted just as good with perhaps a touch of BBQ smoke, lol! Funny time and a great sandwich!

One thing I almost forgot to mention was how great of a travel buddy Kayda was on the trip from Georgia to Indianapolis. Having three younger siblings is not easy. If you can manage being cooped up in the car for 10 hours as we drove across cities and states, oftentimes, with the youngest crying from discontent, you would understand her patience. I know the boys' crying at times drives Kayda-Bug crazy. For months they both couldn't say her name. It is so cute now that her young brother, Ayden, 3 years old, can say her name on demand.

Nathan whenever he sees Kayda will take off waddling to her like a quick-moving penguin. His feet know what to do and to see Kayda embrace him and then he holds her tight warms my heart. Kayda has always been loving towards her siblings although she can set them up for failure sometimes.

One day, we were driving going somewhere. I am not sure to what story or for what. At this time there were only the girls in the car, no boys were born yet! Kayda and Zoe have always recorded videos together. Today, they actually have a YouTube channel called SugarGurls they are launching talking about an array of topics. (Scan the QR to link and subscribe)

Chapter Eight - Kayda-Bug

So on this occasion, the girls had not yet determined to have a channel on YouTube, but they would make videos on their tablets. Kayda decided to do a countdown to begin recording like how you see in movies with the "3, 2, 1, action." I assure you there is a laughable element to this because Akira is involved. Akira enjoys playing with her sister and completing assignments given to her by Kayda. She doesn't do the best with following instructions without adding a few things of her own. She decided to start the recording before she began the countdown.

Kayda gave the tablet to her and said, "I will go first." Kayda-Bug had prepared her introduction to welcome viewers to her video. She was going to give a demonstration on how to make the perfect ponytail. Zoe was so excited to have the tablet and get a job in the production.

The two of them are in the backseat of my SUV and I am driving. As we are cruising along the road, Kayda says, "Okay, you have to countdown from 3 to 1. After you get to one, say action!"

Zoe replies, "Okay," and gives her a nod. She pressed the record button and started to count, "Three…two…one–" before she could complete the word "one" to then say "action," I saw a car swerve out in front of me.

To avoid a collision, I slowed down but more abruptly than I preferred and I blew my horn so the driver saw us! Zoe, said "Whooo!" as she lunged forward. She was holding the tablet in her hand but the jerk made her lose it. Zoe slightly bumped her head on the seat in front of her and Kayda instantly started laughing.

Through her laughter, she asked, "Are we still recording?"

Zoe is giggling also and she replies, "Yeah, I didn't get a chance to stop it."

"Pick it up from the floor Zoe so we can see it!"

Akira picked it up and pressed the stop record button. The video kept recording while it flew out of Zoe's hand and landed on the floor. The girls were laughing hysterically at this point because they were so excited they had great content! We watched that video on repeat for at least a week and showed Grandma too.

The only other video that trumps this one is when the girls are singing a song together in the living room. My children are pretty animated and they love to have fun. My boys can be a bit busy and do things intended good outcomes that don't always pan out. So Kayda and Zoe are singing their hearts out and doing a great job mind you.

My oldest son, Ayden, decides he wants to get in on the song, only the girls quickly give him the "shhhh" face. They like to have their solo parts and he didn't sing on key or know the words. Ayden kept playing with his pig piggy bank that I had got him some months prior. I like little toys that help young people learn. This toy was a pretty heavy pig that you insert large coins into for the

Chapter Eight - Kayda-Bug

pig to count to 10.

The pig was full of these plastic coins and Ayden decided to toss this heavy pig into the air. Mind you, the girls are busy singing their songs, they are paying him and his game no mind. Kayda went through her head back to enjoy her big note and "blame!" she was knocked in the head with the piggy bank.

Silence fills the room and we all look to her to inquire if she is alright. She grabs her forehead and starts to rub it increasingly fast. She doesn't cry, because I forgot to mention, that we were recording the singing session. Kayda-Bug was not going to have herself in tears while she was on video. She tucked her head down and continued to nurse her head.

Zoe at this point can't keep the laughter in anymore and she starts laughing. Ayden, when he heard the "pop" his eyes got huge as he looked at me seemingly frozen in place. He wondered if he needed to run for his life, and I assured him he was good. It was an accident a very tragic accident.

Kayda recovered and went off-camera, I had stopped the feed slightly after the hit but I don't think Kayda knew that. After we were able to calm Kayda's anger down, she wanted to see the video. After seeing the video, she roared into laughter and hasn't been able to stop watching it. We shared the YouTube video with our friends and family members. Man, I was in tears because I was laughing so hard and so did everyone.

CHAPTER NINE

Kayda has such a contagious laugh. One time she was in my room being her sweet silly self, and she was laughing hysterically. I told her, "Breathe Kayda. Calm down before you hurt yourself." Not soon after, she was looking as if her windpipe had cut off. She was no longer laughing just grasping for air it seemed. I was nervous at first because I wasn't sure what happened!

As she calmed herself, she was able to trigger her breathing. We all knew after that to not work her up too much! But it is so hard not to! Kayda is such a fun person and she will do anything to help someone. I remember we were leaving my aunt's house once. Whenever we go somewhere with the boys we have to

Chapter Nine - Kayda-Bug

take seemingly tons of bags, especially when they were younger.

You need extra clothes, socks, bibs, diapers, wipes, cups, snacks, and so much more. They had a bag, I had a bag. At the time, the youngest one didn't walk well enough to be on the ground outside and hold my hand. So, I picked up the baby, carried one of the bags, and asked Kayda to grab the other one. Zoe had picked up our to-go plates.

We always leave my aunt's house full and today was no different. The big difference this night was it was sprinkling outside. I told the girls to hurry up and get out of the rain, but be careful so they don't slip. I quickly got into the car and held the van door open for Kayda. I think she forgot something inside because she went back inside. Moments later she reappeared and she was doing a light jog.

As she got to the end of the driveway, I saw her lose her footing and slip by the front passenger door. She didn't pop back up as I was expecting, so I got nervous and thought to get out of the van. She had lost the items in her hand but amazingly nothing fell out of their packaging. I hollered out of the window, "Kayda can you get up? You okay?"

She seemed to be laying there for a few seconds and I thought did she bump her head on the ground? 'Oh Lord, please don't say we got to go to the hospital.' Then all of a sudden she pops up and starts gathering her items. As she repeatedly says, "Sorry Mom, I didn't mean to take so long," I tell her, "You are fine. What happened?"

She jumps in the car and says, "Mom when I slipped, I think I passed out for a few seconds! I didn't hear or see anything it seemed like for 5 seconds. How long was I on the ground?"

"You were down there for a few seconds because we didn't see you. It was like I saw you and then you just disappeared. I thought you were going to get right back up when you fell. But you didn't. So I was about to get out of the car to try and help you, but you got up and started picking up stuff. Are you sure you are alright? Did you bump your head?"

Akira in a hurried voice says, Kayda are you okay? Shockingly, she was not laughing and neither was I. We were both really concerned and I think shocked.

Kayda replies, "I am fine. I don't think I bumped my head, and if I did I don't feel it. I don't feel any pain. Just wet where my pants hit the ground. Dang, why am I always getting dirty? "

"I told you not to wear those shoes in this weather. Wedges are not the go-to shoe for you in the rain"

"Yeah, I believe you now," Kayda said as she giggled.

Kayda has been a lover of my shoes since she was a little girl. I have pictures of her dressing up in my shoes and walking around like a little lady. To this day

Chapter Nine - Kayda-Bug

she will raid my closet and try on heels. To be honest she had a few crips, where her ankles were as firm as jello in my shoes. Now at 12, I can say she can wear a low-impact heel with no problem. It was so much fun shopping for her first pair of heels for her 12 birthday!

I always try to make her birthdays fun each year. We have been to arcades, in-door play rooms, jumping houses (where you jump on trampolines and such), taking her shopping, and of course, throwing her parties with family and friends. This year will be different because, after 12 years, I have never missed her birthday.

This year she is going to stay with her father for a year! I am happy for her because she has not seen him for two years because of Covid. Normally she goes for the summer and holidays, but with the country on lockdown, it didn't happen. I know he and his family must miss her a lot.

It won't be easy seeing her leave in May, but I know it is time. I told her when she was 13 if she wanted to spend a year with her dad she could. Well, this is that year! I am so glad last year we had so many good times. Something Kayda and I love to do is ride horses.

There is a farm up the street from us, Brogan Farms, and the family is so helpful, loving, kind, and neighborly. They are always allowing children and their parents to see, pet, and ride horses. It was a complete blessing to receive the invitation. I pray that more children get the chance to see the workings of a farm. To see live chickens, pigs, horses, and even goats is always a good time!

K. Lee

My children love hanging out with the livestock and the girls are natural riders. They are more brave than I am when it comes to trusting a horse. I am still timid around horses, but I love to groom them. Brushing their hair and taking out spiky, prickle bushes is my specialty.

Kayda can jump on a horse and ride around for as long as you allow her. She knows how to walk the horse and help her siblings manage the horse, and she wants to advance to a faster horse. I am still a bit nervous about that but she looks great on a horse. I am so impressed with how much she has taken to them because Kayda-Bug is a cautious little person. If she feels nervous or uncomfortable, she is quick to pull away and do something else.

I love that she was so brave she rode the horse through a humongous water puddle. I am not going to mislead you, I didn't do it. I felt like the saddle was too loose for me! I don't see myself wanting to fall into the mud and be soaking wet with the bipolar weather that is present in Indiana. The number one thing I like to do is ride 4-wheelers. I have the most fun and to feel the breeze in my hair and against my back feels like flying. It doesn't hurt sometimes I literally fly off the seat when I hit a bump–exhilarating!

Now I don't try and pop wheelies and stuff, that is too much for me; or spit up mud and such. I just like the cool breeze and open field. So knowing Kayda-Bug is leaving at first made me sad because I know we all are going to miss her. I can only imagine what her dad's side

Chapter Nine - Kayda-Bug

has felt these past two years. It scares me to think of my life without seeing her more often than not.

I am going to miss her and Zoe pretending they are sleeping when I see them with their blanket huts. They prop their blanket up on Akira's bedpost and they go underneath it. I hear the tablet sounding and I know they aren't sleeping. When I open the door, they close their eyes and quickly shut off the tablet. Sometimes I walk past their door and just listen…

I love hearing them giggle and laugh with each other. Although they argue sometimes even most of the time, I know they are truly best friends and love each other. I know the boys will miss her too as will my aunt and grandma.

My Auntie Wendy loves to bake with the girls. They enjoy making cookies and cupcakes, their favorites, with real strawberries and whipped icing. It amazes me how talented these two girls are with a spatula. The boys are not that into baking only eating the final products!

It will be strange to sit at the table and not see her face there or go bike riding and have my bike back. She took my bike because she said she liked mine more, and I needed a different bike that had a peg in the back to hitch the boys to the back tire. I love their caddy, but normally I pushed it instead of dragging it behind my bike. I barely rode my bike because Kayda was using it and so my bike became hers.

So it is time to pack! Her dad didn't ask for

much, which is good, because she is growing fast. Every season is a new wardrobe change and he is happy to be part of the next one. Kayda and I love shopping together and discovering her style. To be honest, she wants to dress just like me and I am so honored. I am a business casual kind of dresser, so to see my child with a blazer on is so impressive.

    I am grateful that she has allowed me to teach her so many things. One of our ongoing projects is the girls will be launching their online store for girls called SugaGurls.com! Kayda and Zoe have always had a mind for business.

    I have been an entrepreneur since the day they were both born. I don't know how not to be creative and how not to crave being my own boss. The girls stayed up with me for hours many times searching for products, filling out spreadsheets (yes they know how to fill them out!), and typing up documents for me.

    Kayda-Bug has turned into quite the editor when it comes to editing videos. I am glad we have special projects we can still work on while she is gone. It always amazes me how children grow up before their mother's eyes. One day they are walking and it seems the next, they are shopping for their shirts, pants, and shoes with a clear sense of fashion.

Chapter Nine - Kayda-Bug

K. Lee

CHAPTER TEN

I am so proud of the young lady I am sending to spend time with her father. Packing her suitcase was hard and to be honest, I had to take a moment a few times to gather myself. I don't want her to be scared to leave, and I don't want her to think my tears are from pain. They are not, but of love, because I love my baby!

I booked the ticket for us three to fly to Florida in mid-April. This will be the first time Zoe is on a plane and the first time I get to fly with Kayda. She has flown before with her father, but not with me. We are planning a girls' trip! So we have our bags packed and we are ready to head to the airport!

Chapter Ten - Kayda-Bug

I thank the Good Yah (Lord) above for blessing me with a family that can drive. We are taken to the airport by my Grandfather. Granddaddy is always willing to help when he can, how he can. The ride was packed with laughter and I was relieved because I needed it.

We got to the airport and the girls' eyes, especially Akira's were wide open. She was excited about boarding the plane. I made sure we had gummy bears, gummy worms, and gum to help with the air pressure. That is one of my only pet peeves with flying, clogged ears! I learned this trick from a man on a plane years back. He told me to hold my nose (like when you go underwater) and blow as hard as I can.

When I blow out, I can feel the air leaving my ear! It is fantastic although, lately, it only seems to work for one side. So for the other, I try yawning and doing anything to push the air out. As we sat at the gate, we made it through security without a problem. Zoe was a little surprised she had to take her shoes off. I told her there was a long story to that.

The announcer comes on the radio, "It is now time to board flight–" How many times have I heard this voice and the excitement instantly builds up in my stomach and a smile hits my face? I haven't been back to Florida in like 10 years! I would like to see some of my friends, maybe go to a mall or two, and just relax. But I forgot to mention, on this trip, the girls and I are attending a gala!

I will be receiving a U.S Presidential Volunteer award and I couldn't be more psyched! It is always good to give back to people and communities. It is an honor to be recognized for something I love to do and would do even if no one notices. So we get on the plane and I watch the girls squirm as the different heights are reached. We break out the snacks and they seem to help. I was glad.

When we landed in Flordia, wow! The weather was beautiful! It was sunny, nice and hot. Perfect weather for being happy! We checked two of our bags so we went to claim them. As we took the journey on the shuttle, we talked about the sites around us. It felt like we were on a second plane full of windows because we could see everything! It is a nice ride.

I don't know how baggage can move so fast, but when we got to our terminal our luggage was already circling on the belt. We grabbed our bags and called Sister Kim! Sister Kim is more like Aunty Kim. She and my mom are really good friends. We practically grew up in front of her. I had missed her as I had not been back to Florida in years. It was so good to see her and I was glad she was able to make time to spend with us.

While with Aunty Kim we ordered pizza, had juice, and watched a few of our movie classics. Oddly, we love Christmas movies even though we don't celebrate the holiday. We oftentimes watch several movies from this season out of the season too! We decided to have a spa day after, and we painted each other's nails and did one another's hair. Funny how Kayda-Bug can style my hair better than me now!

I know she won't have any issues maintaining

Chapter Ten - Kayda-Bug

the style she wants. Zoe is my expert at twisting hair. If I ever want two strain twist, she is who I go to! After several hours of girl time, the girls chose to play their games while I rested. Aunty Kim rode us to our hotel the next day where my good friend, like my sister, TC was waiting for us.

She and I have clicked since we first met. Something about her, perhaps it is because we are both a lot the same. Bishop Martin says we are both alpha females, but I think we both have humility so we listen to each other. I appreciate her advice, company, and friendship!

We plan to spend a night with her on Thursday as we prepare for the gala on Friday night! TC is an expert planner and we get to see what it is like to be in her world firsthand.

The girls enjoy learning new things and having fun while they do it. They helped me pack my books, and want to help me run my booth before the gala begins They are comfortable with handing out business cards, pitching sales to potential customers, and being an all-around help!

So as we dress up in our nice ball gowns we are all breathtaking with our different styles. Zoe with her princess flowing dress, earrings, and matching necklace is beaming with joy. Akira has always loved wearing dresses and dress shoes. I never have to beg or ask her to put on a dress. A dress is like her first move if we are going somewhere.

K. Lee

Kayda tried on the dress we got her from the store and she looks amazing. Unfortunately, because of Covid protocols, many of the dress rooms are closed. So we have to guess sizes and pray they work out. We are pretty sure it would fit nicely and if it didn't I did have a backup dress in case.

But her dress is a pretty floral pattern. Her hair is pressed like she wanted it to be, we recently took out her locs. She wanted to do a blowout and press it and it looks gorgeous! Her hair is super long I do pray that her father can handle it. She has a great head of hair, that is thick and healthy. When I was a child my hair was the same way. I felt like a mushroom when I would have it curled down.

When I was a child, we weren't flat ironing our hair so straight like today. I had some stiff volume so my hair was more like a soft helmet! After we finished working our booth and helping TC, being her legs and feet, we were ready to eat! I love that the gala served a three-course meal. Zoe is more of my vegetarian child. She loves a good salad and would choose it over any meat. The only thing she loves more than salad is corn!

Kayda and I love a bit of everything. I enjoy a mixed array of food, but on this night I elected for the salmon and Kayda-Bug did too. The night seemed to be a fairy tale. The girls and I chatted with TC as each course hit the table. I love tea, so that was my beverage of choice plus the room was freezing. Hot tea always warms me up! Kayda likes iced tea and Zoe prefers juice.

Chapter Ten - Kayda-Bug

We enjoyed each other's company as we always do. Then it came time in the ceremony to call up each of the honorees to receive their award. It was a pleasure to hear the speakers encouraging words leading up to reciting the honorees. We don't always know how our story, or commitments to serve others, really do matter. My goal has always been to make an impact on society, and I am grateful I can do so!

It was a great time taking pictures with my daughters. We had no boys and they ate up every second. We looked gorgeous and felt great. I pray that I can do this more, and host events for young girls to attend with their mothers.

I could host a banquet or a few to encourage bonding between mothers and daughters! I thought to myself. I was really having a great time on that night. It took me a little bit to realize that today was also the last night I would be with both of my girls for several months.

The two of them were quiet on the way to the hotel. Very different from usual. Zoe and my flight had changed from early morning to late afternoon. I would love to spend more time with Kayda, but I do feel like it is time to hand her off to her dad so she can enjoy the daylight with him too.

It will be a bittersweet bye-bye for now. I know this salutation is not for always but a time. Truth be told, I always cry when I leave my babies even when it is for vacation! Don't tell them though.

My children are the biggest part of my life, had it not been for them I don't know where I would be. Kayda, my oldest has been with me for 12 years and I really can't remember a time when she wasn't with me. Her presence in my life brings me so much joy. That joy is more profound than any frustration we may have. Her smile still lights up my heart.

That light is what I know I will remember when I feel that she is distant, and if the power is too strong I will just send her a text from time to time. If she thought her phone was silent before, she will certainly have calls or a text regularly from me.

So we packed up our things, and we walked out to the lobby. Her dad is already here and excited to receive her. He waves and says, "Hey, how's everyone doing?" We all respond with mixed emotions.

Kayda turns to Zoe and me and she tries to hold back tears but I know they will fall. I know she will miss us and may cry from time to time. She hugged Zoe first and said, "You know you are still my best friend?"

Akira is turning pink like she does when she attempts to hold back her tears. Her tears start to fall and she is trying not to let out any loud noises. Kayda hugs her again and she wipes her eyes with her arm, "I know…I am just really going to miss you. Who is going to play with me now? Who am I going to play online with and–"

"Akira I still will have internet and we will play online. We can always video chat and you can call me. Just not when I am in school." Kayda starts to laugh.

"Okay," she replies as she releases more tears. Kayda looks toward me and hugs me. I am a bit out of sorts, and

Chapter Ten - Kayda-Bug

my tears are dropping as I see them say goodbye to each other. I told my Kayda-Bug, "I want you to embrace every experience and have all the fun you can with your dad, siblings, step-mom, and family. I am so excited for you, and no matter what, I am here for you. You can always call me, always text. You can always email, or direct message me too."

Kayda starts giggling. I look her in her eyes and I say, " You are never a bother, and I will always be your mother. If you feel like you have no one, know that is a lie. Your parents are here, your siblings are here, and the rest of your big family too! You are beautiful Kayda-Bug and I love you so much!" I give her another big hug and kiss her on her cheek and forehead as I wipe more tears away.

"I am sorry for crying, I tried not to but I got the can't help it." We three started laughing and I told her, "I got something for you!" I pull the bag out that I had been holding since Indianapolis. I tell her to go ahead, you can open it now. Inside the bag is a wrapped gift. Kayda peels back the wrapping and sees the cover of her first book!

She says to me, "Mom this is my book?" "Yup, this is your first book!" I said. "I told you, I want you to share your stories your way. I want you to write your truth, adventures, about your fun, and the lessons you learn! I would love to read the second book and help you finish it."

She gives me a big hug and says, "Thanks so much, Mom. I can't wait to read it! I really am excited and I don't know what my first book will be about, but I am excited. I gotta go, mom."

"We know, we love you Kayda, and have fun. Nice to see you again Davis, please give my regards to your family. Bye-bye for now Kayda." She turns to walk towards her eager father awaiting her luggage and hand. They were two happy glow bugs walking out of the sliding doors. The air for Kayda felt different as she hit the sun for the first time knowing she wouldn't have to leave in a month or two. She was eager to see her old friends and make new ones.

She missed her siblings and cousins so much while she was gone. Now, she is set on making up for lost time and doing her best to pick up where Covid and life intervened. She is not certain about the next book's topics but she is ready to embrace the journey. Until next time, bye-bye for now readers.

Chapter Ten - Kayda-Bug

Kayda is a remarkable individual, excelling in writing, academics, and entrepreneurship. Her loved ones hold a special place in her heart, and she cherishes spending quality time with them. Kayda's desire to aid children in navigating difficult conversations and emotions stems from her compassionate nature. Despite the challenges of growing up as a young woman, she remains determined to overcome any obstacle.

Kayda's motto, "If you put your heart and mind to something, you can achieve anything," reflects her

About the Author - Kayda-Bug
unwavering determination. She encourages others to persevere in all their endeavors, whether it be making friends, having fun, or launching a business. Kayda is grateful to have accomplished everything she has set out to do and is currently working on her first Roblox YouTube series on her channel SugarGurls.

Scan the QR code to delve into the adventures of her Roblox character and explore her story.

About K. Lee

Krystal Lee is proud to have authored this book and accompanying course to better the lives of readers. She has a heart to help people in their deepest times of need. She writes because she believes there is power in sharing stories and life accounts, that others can benefit and learn from. Sharing is caring, so she shares stories, ideas, and resources to better the lives of her readers.

In addition, Dr. Lee has authored over 20 books across seven or more genres (adult, children, youth fiction, self-help, spiritual growth, novels, and more), in addition to ghostwriting and editing more than 15 published works. She has launched coaching programs, web courses, and helped in the formulation of many startup companies. Her specialty lies in aiding coaches, creatives, and service-based companies in defining their message, brand, unique selling point, client avatar, and generating a sales cycle and structure for her clients.

Empowering individuals is at the core of her work, and she is driven by her passion to continue writing. In addition to being an author, Krystal Lee is a business owner of multiple companies, a consultant, an ordained chaplain, and a speaker.

For more information about Dr. Krystal Lee or to engage with her further, please scan the provided QR code. To engage with the Coaching series and Monthly Meet up Group for Embrace Your Crown First Sundays at 4pm, please use the QR code or visit KLEembrace.com

Shop Books from AuthorKLee.com

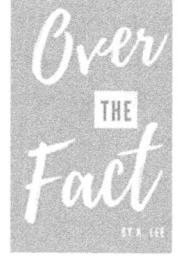

Explore over seven different book genres, and find something suitable for every member of the family.

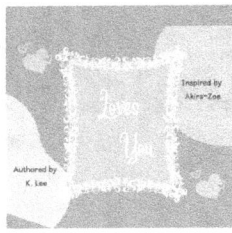

Scan to Shop All Titles by K. Lee

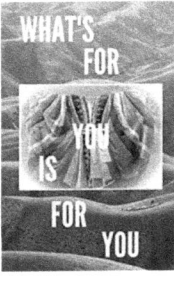

SCAN ME

It's time to start and finish **YOUR Story!**

KLE Publishing specializes in helping people become authors. In as little as 15 to 90 days, we can help you develop your book and publish to 39,000 outlets!

Ghostwrite, Edit, Format, Publish
We can help from
Start to Finish.

KLEPub.com Store

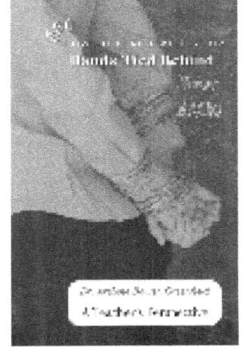
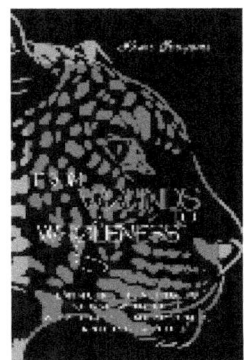

www.ingramcontent.com/pod-product-compliance
Lightning Source LLC
Chambersburg PA
CBHW052114110526
44592CB00013B/1606